Me and My Worry Monster

Snapshots of A Life Lived With Anxiety
And 9 methods to deal with it

By

Wendy Eliot

ISBN: 979-8-9861057-8-9 COPY RIGHTS

Disclaimer

Neither the publisher nor the author is engaged in rendering professional advice or services to the reader. The ideas, suggestions, and procedures provided in this book are not intended as a substitute for seeking professional guidance.

The information presented is the author's opinion and does not constitute any health or medical advice. The content of this book is for informational purposes only and is not intended to diagnose, treat, cure, or prevent any condition or disease.

Please seek advice from your healthcare provider for your personal health concerns prior to taking healthcare advice from this book.

Neither the publisher nor the author shall be held liable or responsible for any loss or damage allegedly arising from any suggestion or information contained in this book.

Dedication

This book is dedicated to my grandchildren,
Tyler and Eadie

Quoted by Tyler

Peace at Last

Table of Contents

Foreword

I was thrilled to accept Wendy's invitation to write the foreword to her book. I'm her twin sister and we have both travelled through the personal development and alternative health field together since Wendy was my birthing partner when my daughter came into this world. She helped me by applying the hypnosis technique she had initially learned from a book and as is her pragmatic nature, she used it on me.

This little book of tips on dealing with anxiety are all a range of things Wendy has used to help her deal with the sh*t life has sent her way.

It's also an insight into the stuff that has shaped Wendy and the snapshots she gives of her life are a window into Wendy's soul as she has evolved through the trauma of being in a cult to the woman she is today.

These take you through both Wendy's work life situations and personal life. I thought I knew my sister and yet she shares here things that she's never shared before.

Each snapshot of some of the traumas she has worked through shows a different insight. Lots of people know Wendy as a professional capable woman not knowing the internal struggles she was dealing with at the time.

Wendy gives a practical action to take after each insight into her life. This is really mind body and spirit and shows how Wendy has used each approach in her soul's journey.

I know this book will touch lots of people who also have their own hidden traumas. I hope that as Wendy shares her most private moments that the reader will be able to use these gifts to help them onward in their own soul's development.

Lynda Cooper RN MBA sister and mother.

Chapter 1

What is Anxiety and What's All The Fuss About?

How many times have you heard someone say "Get over yourself," "just take a deep breath and get on with life."

Well for anyone that's experienced anxiety it would be amazing if it was as easy as that.

I know it wasn't easy for me – at least for much of the time.

I'm a nurse and a teacher, that's what I do. Which means that I'm supposed to be the one that's strong for the other person. I'm meant to be able to walk the talk.

Well, I can walk the talk as far as physical health goes. I cannot remember the last time that I saw a doctor. But unfortunately, this is anxiety I'm talking about, the mind stuff that leaves me doubting myself and my decisions.

So who is this book for?

This book is for those people who have experienced anxiety but don't want to bother anyone with it.

This book is for people who may not even realise they are anxious but just feel nervous at doing something different.

This book is for those who get a queasy stomach before exams.

This book is for those who get 'Sunday night nerves' at the thought of going back to work on Monday.

This book is for those who choose not to do something in case they make a fool of themselves.

This is for those that reach for the wine glass as soon as they get home, because they deserve it, because they've put up with all of the days stress at work.

This book is for those who are in a job they hate but worry about doing something different.

This book is for those who feel they are different to everyone else, and nobody quite understands why they feel how they do.

This book is for those who have that little devil sat on their shoulder whispering all sorts of commentary to stop them doing something out of the norm.

This is for those who get worried when they see people in masks.

This is for those who get worried if people are not wearing masks.

This is for anybody who at any time in their lives has been worried about a future event.

So who am I and what do I know about anxiety?

I'm Wendy. I'm an ex-nurse, ex-nurse teacher, NLP master practitioner and trainer, and spiritual counsellor.

I'm a spiritual being come down for this earthly experience. I have been known to laugh with my contemporaries (and you are one of them) and say – I never realised how thick this gloop down here is, and how easy it is to get caught up in the emotional crap. I've tried practically every self-help method for dealing with life. Some of which I'm going to be sharing with you.

After all what's the point in me knowing about it and not sharing it?

You do not need a qualification. You do not need a certificate. All you need is the willingness to put into practice a few ideas and techniques to see if they work for you.

I don't know you, but I know your energy. You have been drawn to this book for a reason.

I am writing this book for a reason (because my guides showed to me this as one of the many things I can do on my mission to help the world raise its vibration) I sit here alternating between being petrified what people will think and then not giving two f*cks.

This book is written to help you realise how insidious anxiety is and how it debilitates you and prevents you from living the life you were born to live.

We are not meant to suffer. We are not meant to worry. We ARE meant to live with a sense of purpose and divine knowing. (I confess to not being able to stay with this consistently. I know this book was sent to me as a divine action, but it doesn't stop me procrastinating when it comes down to getting it written. You may be pleased to know that I am getting a lot better.)

So, what's happened in your life today to set you off worrying and stressing? Here are a few possibilities.

Have you received a bill you cannot pay?

Have you been given news that a member of your family is not well?

Have you fallen out with your partner?

Have you had trouble at work? Or if not trouble, worries that someone will discover a minor misdemeanour? (I worked in a call centre for a while. The idea that every mistake I made was recorded for posterity really blew my mind)

Has your child/son/daughter messaged you with a problem you feel immediately obliged to respond to?

All of these just add to the feeling of overwhelm and stress which can lead to anxiety, triggering your hormones and inviting you onto the fight or flight fun ride. As you read through this book you will discover that there are a range of ways for dealing with this. For now, let's just explore anxiety in a little more detail.

What is anxiety?

Essentially and very simply –

It is worrying about a future event or consequence that has not yet happened, which then triggers a physical response as though it is happening.

It is a state of apprehension, uncertainty, and fear resulting from the anticipation of a realistic or fantasised threatening event or situation, often impairing physical and psychological functioning.

My experience of anxiety – my head is full of worries; it finds every catastrophic outcome in any given scenario.

I'm not aware of this though – all I feel is my heart palpitating, my stomach churning my body taken over by fear, and my mind beginning to run amok.

I know that it is totally illogical, but that doesn't stop me feeling anxious.

I also recognise some of this comes from my need to do things right! (Thanks dad). So I am constantly judging my actions and often finding them wanting. Being willing to have a go and not get it perfect is a sign of how much I have progressed. The joy when I realise that I am unperturbed about a situation that once would have sent me into panic mode is amazing.

I recognise (though many would be gobsmacked that it's even part of my personality) that I want to please people. I want to fit in. WTF fit in? – but with my beliefs and values – it is highly unlikely that I will fit in with the majority. I was born a maverick, in my head if not in actuality and that internal conflict beautifully sets me up for worry and anxiety.

I want to avoid conflict, but don't want to agree, so I disassociate from the situation, and make up what I think someone thinks about me, and then just don't link to them because after all, I already know what they're thinking (pmsl NOT!) Oh, the joys of how to create anxiety.

So, let's explore the structure of anxiety.

It is a feeling created in your body by the anticipation of a future event.

It is not in the moment. If it was, it would just be a response to a stressful experience. Your brain is amazing and can do amazing things. It experiences your thoughts as though they are real. So when you worry about a possible future scenario, your brain does not know that it isn't real, and your body then responds as though it is. Think of when you have watched a horror movie that's kept you up all night and you just can't get that needed sleep no matter how you try. Your body is responding as though the movie was real.

When you worry, your stress hormones go into action, your adrenal glands begin pumping hormones into your system and set off the "fight or flight" response. This sends energy to your muscles and your body gets ready to run or fight. It withdraws blood from your major organs, and you are left with a survival reaction.

That's fine if it only happens when you are under genuine threat (like with a gun against your head), but as a response to an imagined event, this isn't what you need. In fact, it's doing the opposite, it's putting a physical strain on your body. Stress hormones are survival hormones, and your body is not designed to cope with a constant stream of them.

The mechanism of your survival hormones is a key bodily function for when there is a genuine threat. If it's in response to an imagined scenario then it's not so good. Your body experiences the stress as though it's in the battlefield, it stays on high alert, and is prevented from linking into the natural healing mode which occurs when your body is relaxed and unstressed.

It would take an amazing sage/wise woman or practitioner to be able to stay in relaxed and healing mode in the middle of a war zone.

Yes, it can be done but please don't ask me to do it.

How do you know when you are and when you are not in anxiety?

When you are not in anxiety:

You respond calmly and kindly to whatever is happening around you

You live in the present moment so what might happen tomorrow is of no consequence.

When you are In anxiety:

You imagine a multitude of scenarios that could go wrong.

What if they listen to that call where I flirted?

What if I've forgotten to do DPA and they hear that call? OMG I've repeated myself so many times today – did I tell them all calls are recorded?

And the hormones go into action.

Doesn't matter if you did or you didn't – just worrying about it f*cks up your immune system.

I have a name for the part of me that feeds my anxieties. I call him the worry monster.

It is the part of me that reinforces all my limiting beliefs about myself. It's the part that whispers in my ear all of the possible negative consequences of anything I might say wrong or do wrong. It's the part that feeds any slightly negative thoughts and builds them into a mountain. It's the part that is self-critical and demeaning.

Throughout the rest of this book, I will highlight at the end of each chapter the thoughts and beliefs that the worry monster was feeding me at each point in time. This will enable you to assess your own thoughts and processes and possibly recognise some familiar myths you tell yourself.

I will follow it with the philosophical and spiritual truths that when accessed can slay the monster. These may seem unusual when you first read them and are the basis of spiritual practice based on faith in spiritual truths. They don't even need to be "true" in the form of evidence, but if you live your life from the perspective that they could be true, it will create a very different internal dynamic for you.

Following each chapter will be an activity that can help you to bring your worry monster under control. Each activity has helped me in my progress through this journey called life. Some have been more beneficial than others, but all have helped in some way. I encourage you to give them a go and see what works for you. Reading about them is not the same as putting them into practice.

I wish you well in slaying your worry monster.

The first activity is that of setting a calm anchor or trigger that you can activate to help you remain calm.

Lynda, my twin sister, used this technique before going into a court hearing.

ACTIVITY 1

Setting a calm anchor

What is an anchor you may ask? It is the trigger for a conditioned response. It may be intentional or unintentional.

We have all learnt about when we can condition a dog to salivate at the sound of a bell. Well we can use this process to trigger a wanted response or feeling in ourselves by accessing a feeling and then setting an anchor to go with the feeling.

Anchors occur without our awareness at times of peak emotional experiences, whether becomes good or bad.

Examples of this are when a certain smell brings back memories, or a favourite song cheers you up.

This particular technique is amazing to use for several reasons

- By practising accessing a feeling that you want to feel it becomes part of your neurology and it becomes a good habit.
- It enables you to learn how to amp up a good feeling.
- It is ideal when preparing for likely stressful situations, like presentations, court hearings, or job interviews.

Technique

The best time to set this is when you are feeling happy and stress free.

Think of a time when you were feeling confident, calm, and serene.

(You can choose whichever feelings have the most impact for you. I looked up the opposite of anxiety and there was a list of over 500 words, chose any 🙂)

Now as you think of that time, what were you seeing, hearing, and feeling. Get really into the emotional state. And be aware of when the emotional state reaches its peak… and then relax.

Now, again, but this time as you fully access that feeling and emotional state, at the same time, connect your thumb and ring finger and apply pressure.

Having done that give yourself a shake down, think of blue elephants and have a little jig.

Now come back and simply apply pressure as you connect your thumb and ring finger.

I recommend the ring finger as you are less likely to do this action unintentionally, or have an anchor already attached to it. Many of us connect our first finger and thumb when meditating or other similar activities, this means it's already linked to certain feelings.

If you have performed the technique accurately you will have found that the feeling is immediately triggered again.

If not, it simply means that the emotional state you have chosen may not be "clean" or you may have applied pressure after the peak of the emotional state.

If you find yourself getting stuck, please feel free to message me via messenger.

You can also use a spoken word to link to the feeling e.g. say calm at the same time as you apply the pressure.

Just remember to have fun.

Chapter 2

Snapshot of A Stressful Job

I am standing in a car park at the end of a long day in a care home which is under duress.

I am in a state of overwhelm and stress and sobbing into my phone to my peripatetic manager who is finishing another job for me before she can come and join me at this care home.

The reason I am crying is I have just spent a day in the nursing home where there are several major safeguarding issues, and the residents are considered to be at risk. The home is under threat of closure and a legal team have engaged me and a colleague, Steve, to help and assist in a turnaround. The plan is for us to improve the systems and care for the residents and prevent the threatened closure.

The local authorities have been very clear that they have doubts about the abilities of Steve and me. Steve is the lead on the project, and I have been engaged for my clinical expertise in care home management.

I have previously been called in to assist many homes in distress. This I can unequivocally say is one of the worst.

The manager is struggling along, covering shifts, working short staffed, with no proper systems of care. She is hostile to our presence and cannot see where there are any shortfalls. The local authorities and CQC (Care Quality Commission) are also sceptical of what can be done. Even the residents' relatives are not impressed by our presence as they do not see what is wrong with many of the outdated practices that are taking place in the home.

All this is fine food for my worry monster. My need to be liked, my need to be seen to be doing a good job, my need to be recognised as competent by others, my need to be "right".

I am normally a friendly kind of person and, contrary to what many may believe about me, I do not like conflict and have plenty of self-doubt. I am used to having good relationships with the local authorities that I work with and have worked hard to build my reputation in the care home management sector. None of this seems to matter to this team.

But thank heaven for Steve, he has faith in me and my capabilities. He models how to work through the process of doing the turnaround whilst helping me stay true to my values.

A previous employer had once told me that when I look in a mirror, I am looking at one of the best care home managers she knows. I have to remind myself regularly of that throughout my time at this home.

At this moment in that car park, this fact has completely slipped my mind. Thoughts are running through my mind. "I'm not even sure I want to be in care home management anymore if this is what it entails." "Why am I putting myself through this?"

Here begins some of my most stressful days as a care home management consultant.

Walking the middle line between local authority teams visiting the home and demanding to know what is happening, whilst also trying to implement new systems in the home, and reporting the results to the homeowners, and sending weekly reports to the local authority and CQC is no easy task.

The homeowners are some of the best I have worked with. They have only recently bought the home and have not been aware of some of the issues. As non-clinicians they had believed the guidance of the manager. They are backing the turnaround team to the hilt and invest in everything we ask whilst supporting us in all actions.

During this time, I develop a very irritable gut. I can genuinely say that this job, in this home, is the best cure for constipation that I have ever experienced. Each morning I get the gripes and have to go to the loo before the start of the day.

I also confess to reaching for a glass of wine with my evening meal at the hotel where I'm staying. Anything to ease the nagging anxiety I am feeling.

I find myself seriously questioning myself and the job I am doing. My makeup is such that I struggle to be blasé about people not appreciating I am doing my best (the local authority staff, the relatives,) I am not used to being at loggerheads with the local authorities and this adds to my distress and self-doubt.

I am spending 5 days a week at the location and it's a nightmare. I bring in my best and favourite manager to cover the day-to-day supervision whilst I continue updating all the systems and all documentation. We work brilliantly together, and I believe we make one of the best teams there are.

This process continued over a period of months, and we finally get to the day when the home is allowed to start admitting residents again and achieved an acceptable audit from the regulatory bodies. Fantastic news, but was it worth the toll?

I look back now and recognise that my temperament may not have been ideal for such work as I do not "thrive on stress" as some people claim to. When I do a job, I have this need to do it "right" and this leads to incredible internal stress when I can't manage to get things "right". I was taking on the responsibility for the whole world (well the whole of the nursing home) and every person living in it, attending it, visiting it, working in it.

This is a majorly clever way in which to create internal stress!!!

Imagine .... My worry monster manifests as self-doubt. He cannot resist whispering negative comments in my ear, pointing out everything that could have been done better and then reminding me of the possible negative consequences. I have an amazing and sometimes irritating knack of being able to see both sides of an argument and even argue against myself at times. This is not the best thinking pattern for a worry-free life.

Thoughts and beliefs from my worry monster

Doubting my own abilities and feeling unable to stand up for my values.

Beliefs:

- you're useless if you can't get this done
- it's your fault if this home doesn't improve
- you have to get it right all the time

- there must be something wrong with you if they don't like you

Truths with which to slay my worry monster

I am not in charge of the world

I am not responsible for the whole of the world

I am responsible only for myself

I contribute to others not trusting me when I don't trust myself

What others think about me is none of my business

I am allowed to make mistakes without beating myself up.

Addendum

At this point I would like to stress that the majority of people working in care homes are there because they care and want to look after the residents. I have worked in many amazing homes (that's why I was able to help these homes in distress).

I have met some absolutely amazing and dedicated staff in every home I have worked in. Those who keep coming to work in the most adverse conditions because they care so much for their residents. I have seen staff buy food and clothing for residents when budgets were being stretched. The respect I hold for these staff is second to none.

The system itself and the systematic reduction in funds, and increase in dependency of residents, means the industry is indeed under huge pressures.

The home was turned around and my peripatetic manager is now working as the regional manager for that group of homes.

Interestingly, the key person who had a strong dislike for me in the local authority was removed from the team shortly after our experience in the home.

ACTIVITY 2

Mindfulness

As I have stated previously, anxiety is future oriented. It is rarely linked to the here and now, because if it was it would be fear of what's happening in the moment.

Mindfulness is about becoming aware of what is happening in the here and now. Bringing to mind the positives.

Technique

Bring you attention to the here and now.

This can be done in several ways

- Become aware of your breathing. Is it rapid? Can you calm it? Are you breathing into your chest or abdomen? Is it even? Is it slow? How can you take control of it?
- Become aware of your body. E.g., is your body connected to the chair? Where is it connected? Are your feet on the ground? What does the surface you are stood on feel like?

- Notice your environment – how many blue things are there in the room? How many cars that are the same make as yours on the road? What can you see, hear and smell?
- Become aware of being aware. e.g., as you are aware of your foot on the cool grass, who or what is it, that is aware of that awareness?
- Complete a full body check for any areas of tension and then let it go. Start at your feet and work up your body allowing each section to then become more relaxed. This is especially good for helping you to get to sleep.

I suggest that you practise all these tools when not in a state of high anxiety, but when either mildly anxious or as a morning/evening ritual.

Mindfulness is particularly good if you just have a feeling of discomfort and are not sure where it is coming from.

Good luck with your practice. Feel free to share your experiences on our Facebook group.

Chapter 3

Snapshots on Health

Ironically this is not a chapter about my ill health but that of my sisters', and the worry I allowed it to create.

The first scare came when my younger sister Anne was experiencing a lot of pain in her joints and her hips. She struggled to climb the stairs at the tender age of 33 and was diagnosed with a condition known as Lupus.

It is an autoimmune condition and can be deadly. Emphasis can be, not will be.

It didn't help that I had nursed a young woman who had this disease, and she was stuck in my memory. When I nursed her, I learnt that a severe form of the disease could lead to death in as short a time period as 5 years, so what did my worry monster do ...it created images of my sister dead and dying and me at the funeral.

I couldn't sleep for nights.

*Note - This is known as catastrophic thinking ... and I was an expert.

It is a pattern of thinking where I create an all singing, all dancing, vision of what can go wrong, and then repeat and replay it to myself consistently. (What's ironic is this kind of thinking when applied to positive images, is a very good way of helping to achieve success)

At this time, I was also beginning to explore holistic health and the notion that we create our own illness, and that illness serves a purpose for the individual. Essentially our body listens in and creates solutions for outcomes we want to achieve.

My example for myself is how I created my hay fever. I was still at school and coming up to taking my O levels, (yes, I am that old). As a healthy teenager I was enjoying a social life that involved going out to various youth clubs on an evening.

Studying for my exams was not my priority. It was however rather important to my parents, and being the little people pleaser that I was, I did not have the emotional resources or assertiveness skills to challenge their expectations. I did have a very strong urge to enjoy my nights out.

My body, being the amazing entity that it is, got me sneezing regularly in the summer sun. What better excuse for not being able to concentrate on studying and for not performing well in an exam. The pattern was learnt and continued for many years… until I was exploring holistic health. As soon as I realised the reason behind my initial symptoms, my hay fever disappeared.

So back to my sister's health. I had a bad habit of thinking I was responsible to make sure that people did what was best for them according to my model of the world, so I tried to tell my sister about this.

Any points for guessing how my trying to impose my beliefs went down. Yep, you get the prize … like a lead balloon!

What I came to recognise is that my sister sorts things in her own way. She does acknowledge how the disease came at certain points in her life, and worsened at specific points later in life… and she also has an amazing ability to continue living a full life whatever is happening with her health

Back to my worry monster … many years later as we were celebrating her 25th wedding anniversary with a renewal of her marriage vows on board a cruise ship, my same worries emerged again, as a specific aspect of the disease had developed for her.

Again, I'd got her dead in 5 years.

I am pleased to report that she has now been married 39 years. (I love it when I'm proven wrong on these occasions,) and her disease is stable.

So, then my twin sister became my next health worry target.

"Wendy I've found blood in my urine, and I know I haven't got an infection." These were the words my twin sister shared with me.

We were both nurses. We knew the implications for this.

We are also part of a family that has a cancer gene. My mother died of bowel cancer and each of her brother and sisters had cancer in one form or another.

My auntie had had bladder cancer, so the family history was repeating for Lynda, (that's if you believe in cancer in the way it is purported in reductionist medicine.)

Me and my sisters are all nurses. We were all well indoctrinated (look at that word again lol) into the medical model of disease. It was at this time that I discovered just how much that indoctrination affected me.

When Lynda was first diagnosed, I could not say the C word. I could not believe how hard I found it to say.

I was a holistic health practitioner!

I was a nurse!

I was above these shortcomings!

But it hit me in the gut every single time I tried to say it. The worry monster took hold. All the negative connotations of the C word came into play. As a nurse I had been exposed to those people who died with cancer rather than the ones who survived. I cared for those with complications or who were too far along the disease process to recover.

To add to my own responses and inner conversations, it was astounding how people reacted when they heard the word cancer, and that triggered every negative belief I held.

Nothing feeds back to me my limiting beliefs more than a shitty health diagnosis for a member of my family.

I got to researching. Lynda and I had come across the work of Dr Hamer when we were learning NLP (Neuro Linguistic Programming) and I went back to that information. It wasn't until later that I found out that Lynda had been too scared to even do the research. (Her experience of the way that health practitioners took on the cancer sympathy expression at every meeting also was a big influence on this.)

It's no wonder so many succumb to the expectations of the medical model.

Dr Hamer's information perfectly reflected the situation that had led to Lynda developing this biological program in her bladder. Thank you Tad James for introducing us to that work sooooooo many years ago.

Knowing how much our beliefs are installed unconsciously over the years, and how long we had been part of the medical establishment, Lynda went for a belt and braces form of treatment, using complementary therapies for the emotional healing and standard treatment to get rid of the growth.

We had a magical experience during this time. Lynda was wanting to release all the hurt and emotional pain that she was feeling. We often work together in a holistic fashion. I was supporting her in this process, and part of the process we were using was to identify where the emotional pain is situated in the body and then use various processes to release it. I was still running with an undercurrent of my own anxiety and feeling the importance of the need for the therapy to be of help. I felt helpless as it was and then came my "oh sh*t" moment, she answered that it was in every cell in her body. I had no idea where to direct her to next, I felt useless and wondered what the next step would be to try. I was never more aware of my limitations as a practitioner and a human being. What could I do?

...but the universe has a way of delivering its own wisdom and the creator directs us to what we need, and Lynda had just that morning been doing a breathwork meditation which triggered an idea in her. Knowing that the blood takes oxygen to every cell in the body and that she wanted to reach and heal every cell in her body, she decided to breathe in love, which is the greatest healer, and breathe out hurt.

All I could do was "hold the space" for her (meaning focus my love and attention on her and keep the intention of the practice in mind.) I watched and brought my breathing into sync with hers. I was amazed when the room started to glow. The light changed to having a pink haze around Lynda. That pink haze stayed with her throughout the process. It was a beautiful confirmation that she was indeed breathing in love. (Pink is the colour associated with love.)

It wasn't only Lynda who healed that day. Seeing the energy and knowing its significance helped to put some aspects of my worry monster to bed and reaffirm my belief in a power higher than mine.

Thoughts and beliefs from my worry monster

Believing in the myth of a family history and genetic influences.

Being influenced by other people's reactions to the C word.

Thinking I am responsible for the health and well-being of those who are close to me.

Feeling the fear created by them choosing not to follow my guidance, which I know can be of help.

Catastrophic thinking patterns which were fed by past conditioning about medicine and health.

Truths with which to slay my worry monster

What I experienced yesterday is not a predictor of what I will experience today.

Allow other people their sovereignty, they have an amazing ability to manage for themselves.

Family history does not have to be my history.

Illness serves a purpose and when you work out the purpose it is likely to enable the body to move into healing mode (it does this naturally unless under stress).

Hold a view that the universe has my back and the back of all my relatives.

ACTIVITY 3

Handover to a higher source

It is said that worrying is a form of negative prayer and when you worry you are requesting what you are worrying about to become a reality.

Higher source does not judge "right" or "wrong". As a spiritual being having a human experience, all experience is considered valid whether it is labelled good or bad.

By worrying, you are demonstrating faith: not in what you want, but in what you fear.

So how can this be overcome?

Connect with your higher self, God, or the universe (whichever resonates for you) and request for the situation to be resolved to everyone's higher good.

And then let it go.

Don't try to think of a solution. Don't try to solve the problem. Simply hand it over. The Universe knows what you do not. It has the connection to each and every person on the planet (even when they are unaware of that connection)

In seeing a positive outcome for everyone concerned you are putting a vibration out to the universe for that outcome without creating any kick back on you. Some people call it Karma. I call it unintended consequences. I believe If it puts someone else down, it is putting you down. We are all connected at source, so in wishing the best and seeing the best in others, you are seeing the best in yourself.

It is so simple and yet such a profound way to hand over your worries.

As with all previous tools please let me know how you got on by recording the results on my Facebook page.

Chapter 4

Snapshot of A Care Home Inspection

Its 10am on the day after the Brexit vote.

I'm sat in my office and the nurse on duty comes to the office door and says, Wendy the CQC are here.

I am due to catch a train at 2pm for a weekend in London. It's the last thing I want to hear.

There goes my trip, I think to myself.

The officer is brought to my office and introduces herself.

I don't know about any other nursing home manager, but my heart races every time these turn up. (For anyone in education, this is the equivalent of an Ofsted inspection.) The inspections are unannounced, and you have no idea they are coming, hence the fact I was going to London.

My worry patterns often make me doubt that I am a good manager, and the inspection process is one that I am always worried about, especially as a registered manager – I know that all that happens in the home is my responsibility by law. It is a responsibility I do not take lightly.

I know my home is a good quality home. I know it is a home where I would put a member of my own family. I know my team come to work because they care about the residents. I know they are capable of exemplary care. I know we have cared for and helped so many residents and yet…I still feel the anxiety.

As the manager I also know the areas that need improvement. Many of these are in the area of record keeping, (any care home managers feeling the empathy here?)

My heart is racing more so on this day as my admin is taking annual leave, my head housekeeper is away on an infection control course, and I want to catch that train!

I was 2 staff down at the start of the shift and had to call in agency staff. My regional manager had left the day before so no one from head office is available to come along for support.

My deputy (who had only been in post a few weeks) was to cover the weekend and had come into the home to take a handover from me. She is an exceptional nurse and practitioner.

My heart is physically palpitating. My anxiety is up at a number 10. My brain is disconnected from thinking straight. I am aware of so many areas in the home that are still a work in progress.

I inform the inspector that I will cancel my train and travel later, but she says, there's no need to do that. She is going to complete the questions with me that I would normally do at the end and then see how things are progressing before I make a decision whether or not to cancel my journey. (I am thrilled to say that I got on that train.)

Throughout the conversation I am aware of all that could go wrong. Good old catastrophic thinking again.

What actually happens is that I am totally blessed. My relationship with the local authority went before me and the Inspector was aware of how we were working in conjunction to improve the home.

All my doubts about how I manage the home are assuaged.

My admin has such wonderful systems I can find everything the inspector wants.

My head housekeeper arrives back from the infection control course, and as my infection control advocate gives amazing details of the systems she has set up in the home.

My nurses are exemplary and ensure that any notes and records are all up to date before the inspector sees them. (Including getting me to sign some that I had forgot to sign)

The local authority had given good feedback on the way in which the home responded to any shortfalls and how we take immediate action.

My handyman has all his health and safety checks up to date.

My staff can tell her what they would do in the event of a safeguarding concern.

My staff provide all the information required even when I am not in the building.

As it comes to the end of my conversation with the inspector, she advises me I'm fine to go and catch my train!

I climb onto the train with a sense of wonder and astoundment at how well the inspection has gone, despite all the possible things that could have gone wrong. I feel incredibly proud of my team.

In my head, at the start of the inspection, it had been a very different outcome. My anxiety about the potential outcome caused me to be at less than my best for the first hour of the inspection. My habit of focusing on the negative and what could go wrong had me in a kerfuffle. A little adrenaline may be good for performance, but the extent that it affected me physically meant I was unable to think clearly.

If my staff had had the same response we would have been well and truly in the kaka. I knew logically that there was no need to feel so anxious, but my body and head refused to behave.

For the record the report result was "good", and my team were absolutely amazing.

Thoughts and beliefs from my worry monster

You should have done more in preparation for the inspection

You are in charge of everything that happens in the nursing home. And that means everything!

CQC inspectors can be horrendous.

It will make your life uncomfortable if the home does not perform well … and it will be your fault.

Truths with which to slay my worry monster

People come up trumps to support you.

People come into care to care.

Being a good role model works wonders.

The staff that surround you reflect you. Be the role model you want your staff to be.

ACTIVITY 4

The what if scenario

My worry monster was famous for all the crap it whispered in my ear …. and I believed it.

Its favourite line is – What if?

What if this goes wrong.

What if the staff don't do this right for CQC?

What if you take after your dad and have a heart attack?

What if you take after the rest of the family and get cancer?

What if.. What if … What if…

And where the mind goes the energy flows and feeds the monster all the more.

When I was looking for different solutions to worry and this was one of the most simple and most profound for me. The truth is that the majority of things we worry about do not materialise and if they do, we are able to deal with them far better than we expect. I can vouch for this for what I have dealt with. I spent more time worrying about "what if" than enough.

So, here's the exercise

Switch the wording to what might go right!

And find at least 5 ways of it going right in comparison to the thought of it going wrong. The reason for this is our brain is programmed to focus on the negative and there is evidence that we require 5 good point for every negative one to get into balance.

We are spiritual beings who create our reality, often out of our conscious awareness. In doing this exercise you are taking control of your conscious awareness and reprogramming and realigning your thoughts.

What if it goes right?

What if the staff behave amazingly well and CQC focus on the positive?

What if they excel and work as well as they always do?

What if the CQC inspector has been given amazing feedback about your home by the local authority?

What if your head housekeeper turns up and tells the CQC all the amazing things she is doing?

What if I don't take after my dad and so I break the generational pattern?

What if its not a generational pattern?

What if I know I am fit and healthy?

What if I don't take after my mum and break the familial pattern?

What if I know that cancer is a biological programme?

What if I know that in the unlikely event of becoming dis eased, I know how to cure myself?

What if? What if? What if?

Our mind is wired to process the negative as a safety mechanism so this may take a little practice, but it can be done.

Lynda has very fond memories of the day I first clicked into this pattern. I walked into our office on a high, and all I did throughout the day was go what if and declare a positive statement. I was like a child with a brand-new toy.

Chapter 5

Snapshots of A Cult Experience

I was in my mid-thirties. A nurse teacher with a daughter and married to a man who is salt of the earth variety and into shooting and wildfowling. On paper I had everything, but I felt as though there was something missing, but I didn't have a clue what. I was interested in alternative health practices and had taken my twin through labour under hypnosis. I wanted a way of keeping fit and healthy that also matched my alternative health and spiritual needs.

I saw an advert for Tai Chi Qigong and wanted to attend. I brought my twin sister along for the interest. I absolutely loved it from day 1. I became totally caught up: in the philosophy; the dedication to the art; the commitment to the practice; to stopping drinking alcohol and to becoming a teacher of this art.

My Sifu seemed amazing. I was totally convinced of Qigongs effectiveness when he did some reflexology on my foot and I physically felt the energy flowing down the side of my head. I was already interested in energy and healing and complementary therapies, so this fit to perfection. The original commitment was meant to be 1 evening a week, but then it stretched to 2 to support other teachers in the group, and then it became more and more.

It became apparent that grading was not only based on completion of the tai chi forms but also in a person's commitment to the organisation. I ended up as the secretary of the organisation with 2 classes of my own per week, plus supporting other classes and attending the office headquarters twice weekly to do the admin. I achieved a black belt and third dan.

Some of the rules were inconsistent and it became obvious that some students were favoured more than others. I worked hard to become a favoured one.

The Sifu had a second in command, and much that I learnt about the art came through her. It was her guidance on how to treat the founder, it was her interpretation of his requests.

She was the one who had a major influence over me. I hadn't heard of a narcissistic personality then, but boy can I tell you about it now.

She went from being an ardent fan of the Sifu to then beginning to question the way he taught us. She was incredibly good at sowing seeds of doubt. She was so close to him that I considered she must know more than me. I was totally besotted with her capabilities: the fact that she also had some psychic abilities intrigued and fascinated me. I fell into the trap of thinking that she must know more than me, that someone with these capabilities was much closer to being awakened than me. I literally worshipped her and her skills. We worked closely on several projects. Such was my uncertainty about my own identity that I never questioned her.

I totally believed that she knew better than me. I was confused by her behaviours at times and now I understand this is typical of someone gaslighting and leads to an undermining in confidence. It was the equivalent of a 1 on1 cult and the way in which it triggers confusion and lack of self-trust.

Her favourite line was "yous can do what you want", implying that anything other than what she suggested would be the wrong decision. I was so unsure of my own boundaries and standards that I went along with all her suggestions.

To cut a long story short, mainly because I don't know how to put it into words without boring you to tears. In the 4 years of being involved, first in the club of Lamas and then in the cult of Maggie: I separated and divorced my first husband; I took redundancy from my job as a nurse teacher and I went into business with my twin - then sabotaged that business for the sake of Qigong. The business failed because I chose to follow Maggie. Some people even thought I was in a lesbian relationship with her. Many commented on how I behaved differently when she was present to when I was running my own classes.

Within the space of 4 years, I had gone from a successful nurse teacher earning an amazing salary to a Qigong teacher living with her mentor, estranged from my family and daughter, and living on benefits.

So, what does all this have to do with anxiety? For those 4 years I lived on the edge of my nerves. I do believe that if I had not practised the Qigong I would probably have had a major nervous breakdown. Instead, I coped. At the expense of my self-esteem. At the expense of my nervous system. At the expense of my mental well-being. At the expense of my family, and my biggest regret: at the expense of my daughter.

The cruellest trick that was pulled on me was when my daughter did visit me, my alleged mentor and friendly narcissistic Sifu, told me that my evil energy would transfer into my daughter if I hugged or touched her.

She had convinced me that I was soiled and my energy corrupted. My daughter was 13 years old at the time. (She loved me unconditionally throughout and I am pleased to tell you she had an innate sense of right and wrong and we are now the best of friends). But the thought that I might contaminate her with my energy prevented me relating closely with her at that time.

Anxiety was my normal state of being throughout this. We would go for a meal out at a local pub and then Maggie Maggot as I now fondly refer to her, would say something to trigger me and I would not be able to eat the rest of the meal. When I finally found the strength to leave the cult of Maggie, I weighed eight stone. All my belongings fit in the back of a Fiat Uno and I lived on a caravan site next to a dog track.

Maggie had abandoned me and moved into a cottage on her own. This meant my family were able to come back into my life and get me out of her influence, but not before a lot of psychological damage had been done.

How was I rescued? …by my amazing family.

My twin sister who had been with me right up to Maggie Maggot creating her own school of Qigong, had never given up on me. She, and some other ex-members of the cult, got together and hatched a rescue plan. I now look back on this as divine intervention.

Lynda tells me that the "how to get someone from a cult" guidelines included keep reaching out to the person and letting them know you are there.

I found myself being invited to lots of family events, and it all culminated on an Easter Sunday.

I was invited to Sunday Dinner at Lynda's home. (I had started having doubts about The Maggot, but believed I had no one to turn to. I had cried myself to sleep in the freezing cold caravan.... so cold the gas pipe froze and there was no heating).

I went for that Sunday dinner and Lynda, my twin sister, looked at me and said "you don't need to be loyal to her anymore" and my whole world collapsed. The front I had been putting on. The debt and despair I was in. The whole kubutz. Me, the once proud nurse teacher, the main wage earner, now in a state of poverty, not earning enough to support myself, never mind my child, and with a self-esteem lower than my boots.

The standing joke in our family is to be careful if you invite me to dinner as I may end up living with you for the year, which is exactly what happened for me with Lynda. Her and her hubby were amazing in how they supported me with getting back into 'real life'.

But no one knows (until now) of the nights I spent crying myself to sleep and still believing that I was evil.

I drummed up the courage to go onto radio, denouncing the Maggie Maggot experience. (She did think she was Christ reincarnate, and I was Judas). And true to my role, I betrayed her and exposed her lies and deception.

There is much about that period of my life that I have forgotten. I have healed many of the wounds I experienced. I have an amazing capacity for negating/forgetting things to such an extent that it was only when my sister reminded me that the Maggot had had me sleep on the garage floor so her son could sleep in my bed that it triggered a few more things for clearing.

How could I allow someone to treat me so poorly?

I've worked out that it's the combination of having high ideals and low self-esteem that allows someone to be vulnerable for recruitment into a cult. The maggot knew what my ideals were and played to them. She knew my need for approval and played to that.

She seemed to read my deepest fears and then come rescue me from them. She read my uncertainty, she read my anxieties, she read me!!!

My worry monster and lack of confidence in myself increased her influence. It backed up every negative notion she installed via suggestion and inference. It allowed her to take me from someone who had a sense of purpose but lacking confidence, to a broken, anxious, worried shell of who I used to be. I now acknowledge that it wasn't her who took me there, it was me who gave her the power to do so.

Throughout this time, I was busy practising and teaching Qigong. As an art that involves breathwork and meditation, it allows my nervous system to calm down and have a break from the constant underlying anxiety. Without it I consider I may well have ended up physically or mentally ill.

What fed the worry monster?

Self-doubt and believing others were better than me.

Self-doubt in thinking that the Maggot knew more about me than I did.

Feeling unable to make a decision for fear of making the wrong decision.

Questioning my own observations about the Maggot and thinking I had it wrong.

Truths that diminish the worry monster

No one knows more about me than I do.

My values are mine and mine alone.

What others think of me is none of my business.

I am now aware that narcissists will use my values against me.

I am now aware that narcissists provide a golden period where they praise you and make you think they care about you. They don't.

ACTIVITY 5

Qigong breathing techniques and a simple exercise to expel anxiety

The Qigong breathing and exercises were what helped me to remain sane and healthy whilst working and living with a gaslighting narcissist. Since recovering from being in the cult and now connecting back to my spirituality, one of the things I am mega pleased about is that one of the guides who channels through me is a Qigong Master.

This has resulted in me being able to feel the energy in a very different way when I am practising for myself or teaching others.

I didn't do any Qigong for a while after coming out of the cult of Maggie, as I associated it too strongly with the way in which I had been treated.

I am glad to say, that association is now over. I have since met the woman in question at a networking meeting. That gave me some nice stuff to release! but also helped me realise how far I have come. I don't identify as a victim anymore. I am no longer unsure of how to react should I see her again. I know me as the powerful and spiritual being that I am.

Worry Monster Qigong Exercise

This exercise can also be found on my YouTube page with a demonstration of the forms.

Firstly – stand with your feet at shoulder width apart, knees relaxed, and arms placed on your abdomen.

Now place the tip of your tongue at the back of your 2 front teeth, gently resting against the roof of your mouth.

Then breathe in through your nose sending the breath down to your abdomen. As you breathe in your abdomen will come out and as you breathe out, your abdomen will flatten (well if it's not got the curves that mine has!) If you watch new-born babies and young children this is how they breathe.

Practice this for a while, gently breathing in ….. and then gently breathing out.

If you have some relaxing music, feel free to play it.

Once you are comfortable with this part of the process you are now ready to advance to the particular exercise I want you to perform.

It was a favourite of some of my students who worked in a care home. When they were feeling stressed, they would take themselves away and practice this.

Stand with your feet slightly wider apart than shoulder width. Bend your knees slightly like sitting on a horse, (if you've got rickety knees just stand comfortably with soft knees i.e. not locked).

Place your arms in front of you with the palms facing upwards, (a bit like a ballet dancer) the elbows slightly bent as though you are holding a large lightweight bowl. Lift the hands up to chest height and then turn them to face forwards as though you are going to push someone away from you. Then push the hands away but keep the elbows bent (that is do not fully extend the arms). Then turn the palms down and gently lower the arms back to the starting position.

Having practised the move, it's now time to synchronise your breathing to the move.

As you raise your arms, breathe in ….. as you push away, breathe out, imagining you are pushing all your cares and worries away. As the arms come down take a gentle breath in and out ready to take a breath in as you next raise your arms and hands.

And repeat for as long as you want.

If you find you are getting lightheaded you are likely forcing the breath and hyperventilating so simply stop, slow the breath down and breath gently.

Good luck and as always feel free to record your experiences on my Facebook page.

Chapter 6

Snapshots of Anxiety When Leaving A Cult

I had been with Maggi Maggot for 4 years.

During that time I had written a Qigong training programme and got it accredited with the Open College.

I'd assisted in helping her set up a charity where she got paid a high salary (it was OK for me to be poorly paid because I could claim benefits as a single mother. Her words.)

I was considered to be her 'weird' right hand woman.

And then the wisdom within started questioning. Not very loudly to start with, but loud enough to just make me question. Her way of challenging me was to imply that she knew more than I did. That she could have done what I did...in getting the training programme accredited.

I was so enthralled that I believed every word...until I didn't.

As I lay in a freezing cold caravan, disconnected from my family, my friends had already left the cult. My loyalty was being well tested. Loyalty was one of my highest values. I now realise that there is only one person to be loyal to and I look at her every morning in the mirror.

I already told you of the family joke of not to invite me to dinner. Let me go into a little more detail.

It was coming up to Easter in 2001. I had gone through the millennium disconnected and separated from my family. I had been embraced by Maggi Maggots family and all I can ever say to them is thank you for the beautiful people they were. My daughter had no idea where I lived. I rarely saw her and only arranged meetings in public places. (She would have been 15 at the time.)

I had been invited to family events. I had attended, on Maggie's advice as I couldn't think for myself by this time, and that's when the sh*t started to unravel. That's when the wondrous being that is my soul started to question.

I was living in a freezing cold caravan, (I was no longer allowed to share accommodation with Maggie Maggot). Those who had been my friends and support within the cult had seen through the insanity and left. I was at my utter lowest. The colleges and institutions which had supported the programmes we had devised had been informed of the unhealthy nature of the organisation and were calling us in for questioning. I knew the end was in sight.

I didn't identify with being Judas (as Maggie thought she was the reincarnation of Christ) but I ended up doing exactly what Judas did. I betrayed her (at least in her eyes).

Lynda had invited me to Easter Sunday Dinner (I think that is kind of important as the main Christian Celebration of the year)

My family (God bless them) had been reaching out and inviting me to lots of family events. I felt incredibly uncomfortable at each of these. I had no idea of my true identity or how I was "supposed" to behave. I had gauged my responses for 4 years on whether Maggie Maggot seemed to approve of my actions or not. I had been immersed fully in her paradigm of what was appropriate or not.

What is mega weird is that some others just never saw it. They thought we were a normal 'Relaxation and Well-being' training body. Several of my students, when I identified we were part of a cult, just refused to believe me.

I now know that one of the greatest achievements of a gas lighter is how charming they are to others. I don't think they could accept that they had been duped so effectively either. (I was incredibly normal when not in the presence of The Maggot.)

Any way back to my departure.

Lynda and Geoff had invited me for Easter Sunday dinner (we are in Yorkshire folks – it's dinner not lunch) and I went.

All of the doubts that had been building up. The many times I'd thought, you can't say that Margaret it's not accurate. All culminated at this dinner. My twin sister put her arms around me and said, "you don't have to be loyal anymore" and I just crumbled.

I sobbed and sobbed. All the people who had been instrumental in getting me "out" were then contacted. My friend Dot, Maggot's son, My sister Anne, and especially important -my daughter Sarah.

I was out!

But that isn't where it ends. 4 years of gaslighting, 4 years of loyalty, 4 years of constant conditioning, do not disappear overnight. Especially as I had had it Instilled that I was the betrayer, I had evil energy in me, I was the lowest of the low.

I look back and remember how many times she asked me if I wanted to end my life (thank f*ck I was strong enough not to take that one on board) though not strong enough not to refuse to sleep on the garage floor, not strong enough to tell her to p*ss off. I remember reading Stuart Wilde as I slept on the living room floor. His book 'Affirmations' is, I believe, one of the reasons why I was able to get through the ordeal.

Back to Lynda, so I took up residence in the "Harry Potter" room. The room under the stairs in my sister's home.

I spoke on radio about how the Maggot thought she was the reincarnation of Jesus. The programmes I had built, the courses I had invested so much of my life into, were removed from each college's programmes. I was instrumental in bringing her empire down, and at the same time all I had worked for.

I put on a front that all was well, whilst still experiencing acute anxiety and worry.

I lived my life on edge: constantly worrying.

Amid all this what I hadn't shared was...some of the books Lynda and Geoff had on their shelves were about Christianity, the Devil and how people were open to being possessed. I had nightmares that I was evil. It created massive anxiety, but I wasn't going to share it with anyone. They might have thought I was crazy.

I remember one night feeling this massive blackness come and encompass me. I could feel it pressing down, and it was terrifying. The only thing that went through my head that I could hang on to was the Lord's prayer. I repeated it and repeated it and repeated it, until finally the blackness let go.

I now perceive that as a psychic attack. My energies were in disarray and The Maggot was p*ssed off at me. I began building up my spiritual strength by being with people who loved me, who listened to me, and who were there for me.

I now know that I am one strong elemental being: not to be f*cked with. I didn't know this at the time and still believed in my limitations.

It was only speaking with Lynda, at a later date, that we recognised the power of a Christian prayer in our country. Christianity being the main faith in the UK ; I had instinctively and spiritually keyed into the key energies around me to call on and protect me.

I also now recognise that the simple intentionality in what I wanted that prayer to activate was a key component of it successfully doing so.

Remember the intention is key. Hold on to that and believe and the rest is inevitable.

The worry monster programming

You are unworthy.

You'll never get over this.

You are basically evil and will contaminate others.

Provide a front to show to others so they don't think you are stupid.

Truths that diminish the worry monster

I am a powerful aligned being.

I have the courage and strength to navigate any situation.

God always has my back.

I have my own back.

ACTIVITY 6

Learn to meditate

Anxiety is a state connected to feelings about the future, and a really good way of overcoming this is to undertake regular meditation.

Meditation is a stage of relaxation that allows you to switch your body back into the parasympathetic nervous system, the one that helps regulate regeneration and healing.

*If you want a little tip for remembering which part of the autonomic nervous system is which – parasympathetic = peaceful, and sympathetic = stressful

(P and p, S and s)

Here is a transcript for you to record onto your phone so you can listen at any time to assist in relaxation. It is a guided meditation on a healing journey which helps you to access the healing resources within you. If practised regularly you will be able to switch to this relaxed state easily and quickly.

Find a comfortable place to lie down, and then play the recording back to yourself, or you can get a friend with a relaxing voice to read it to you whilst you relax. I used this regularly for my mum when she was recovering from surgery. She loved it. She used to say – Wendy take me to my safe place.

Here it is.

Welcome to this healing journey.

Find a comfortable place to relax. You may choose to sit or lie down. Allow your hands to rest gently by your sides and close your eyes…take a nice slow deep breath …

And now…directing your attention to your feet, allow any tension in them to simply drain away…

And as your feet relax bring your attention to your ankles and lower legs, and allow them to relax …

And now bringing your attention to your knees and thighs… allow any tension to drain away

And now bringing your attention to your hips and groin area and gently allow any tension to drain away …

Now bring your attention to your abdomen and back... allowing any tension to gently drain away

And bring your attention to your hands, and allow any tension to simply drain away...and as you bring your attention to your arms, allow any tension to drain away...

And now to your shoulders and neck ... allow any tension to drain away ... as you then direct your attention to your face and jaw – releasing any tension and ... now ... become aware of the top of your head and gently release any tension in your scalp ...

And now slowly scan from the tip of your toes to the top of your head and release any remaining tension ...

You are now ready to go on your journey.

You are in a room with a door and in this room you can leave all of the baggage and cares and worries of everyday life...

Now open the door and you will see a path ... walk onto this path and follow this path until you come to some water ... it may be a stream, it may be a pond, it may be the sea, whatever it is its water that you love, ...now experience this water in whichever way suits you best, ... (Allow a few moments to fully experience the water).

And now it's time to leave the water and take yourself to your safe space, ... and experience this space in a way most suited to you ... this space is here to support you however you need support …….. (Again allow a few moments to fully experience your safe space).

And now it is time to return to the room, leaving your space, knowing it is here with you whenever you may need it… And as you return to the room … look at what you left here and decide which, if any, of your baggage, you want to take with you as you go forward and which you will leave behind that you no longer want… Trusting your inner guidance.

And now it's time to return to the here and now … begin by wriggling your fingers and toes and become aware of the room and the noises around you … Take a nice deep breath and welcome back …

And when you're ready go forward with the knowledge that this space is carried within you and is available to access whenever and wherever you want.

I do hope you have enjoyed this healing journey and wish you health and wellness.

Chapter 7

Snapshot of Wanting Approval

The incident that I am going to explore in this chapter is one surrounding the lead up to telling my younger sister that I was leaving my husband. It is an ideal example of how I used to behave when I had a major decision to make and questioned my own integrity in being able to make the "right" decision. I purposely put it in quotes, because for any of us that have been on this planet long enough, we know, there is no such thing as a right decision without a context of time and perspective to be added to it.

I recognise that my decision making pattern includes one major thing that is destined to f*ck it up, and that is ..... I worry about what other people may think of the decision.

I worry if my family will approve. I worry if they won't approve. I worry if the man on the street will approve (well not actually but I might as well.)

I worry if people will think less of me because of my decision.

I worry if I cannot explain it logically to render support for the decision (yes, I know, why would I need support? but that's all part of the people pleaser game). It's also a reflection of how, at times, I just don't trust my own judgement.

Crazy as it sounds, I was terrified when telling my younger sister of the decision that I had made to leave. In my head, I heard her disapproving the decision. I could see the look that comes across her face when I know she is disapproving. She doesn't have to say anything, she just has a look! I knew how much she liked my husband, and in my mind, I just knew she would disapprove, and it mattered to me!!!

It's February 2020 before the world went mad. My world was already in turmoil. I had spent the last few months taking my time in coming to the decision whether my marriage was over. It was not an easy decision to make. I had been madly in love with my husband when we first met, and I had never envisioned a time when we might not be together.

I had been incredibly happy. I thought we were for life.

I went into business with my sister and that was when the arguments started. There were many factors that indicated an underlying problem. I had chosen to ignore them, bury them and pretend they were not an issue.

These included that I was reluctant to talk to him about my business, (he thought I was being foolish wanting to help people spiritually). The fact that he was not involved in my business. The concerns about my spiritual beliefs and his lack of respect for them. I felt unable to have these conversations with him. Difficult adult discussions about personal issues just didn't take place. I was like the proverbial ostrich burying my head in the sand and refusing to acknowledge the problems.

But separate from that, let me describe the part of keeping my family informed.

The very idea that this was anybody else's business but mine and his, was also anathema to me. I am an incredibly private person (yes, I know I'm sharing a lot here and you've no idea how that takes me out of my comfort zone) and I do not like discussing issues which make me vulnerable. This time, I felt mega vulnerable.

I eventually made my decision: I was going to leave my husband. I did not want my sister to find out from anyone else and wanted to inform her before the event.

It was coming up to my birthday so seemed an ideal time to arrange a get together and update her on family events.

Lynda (my twin) and I invited our sister out for a meal to celebrate. Lynda was aware that I would be letting my sister Anne know that I was leaving my husband. Anne and her husband had an amazing relationship with my ex. He had been a big part of their families lives, so I knew the separation would have a big impact on us all.

Before going to the venue, I could feel my stomach starting to churn. I do not like feeling as though it is necessary to explain myself to others (yes, I know it's child shadow at play, but I didn't know that then). I do not like having to justify my decisions, but I also was keen to ensure I kept both my sisters informed as they are 2 of the most important people in my life.

There is also a big back story to this. This includes how I felt about myself and how I thought people thought about me because of my cult experience.

My hubby had taken to calling me feeble minded and easily influenced. I believe that this was related to my working with my twin sister, my paying business coaches, and my investment in personal development. As I mentioned I chose not to have any grown up conversations as I thought I knew how he would react. It did lead to me questioning my capabilities and whether I was making the right decision. I wanted to please everyone, and I felt accountable to others for what was essentially my decision, not theirs. I was also taking on accountability for how people reacted and knew I would be hurt if they did not approve or react in the way that I would prefer.

Why did I feel such a need for approval of my decision? Because I had never envisioned being in this position. Because I was unsure of the future. Because I wanted people to agree with my decision. Because self-doubt is part of my human design. Who truly knows? certainly not me!

So back to that day in February 2020. We arrived at the restaurant and my heart was beating rapidly. My mouth was dry, and I felt like I was going to be judged and found wanting. If I had been going to court, I don't think I could have felt more nervous.

Throughout the meal I went through the motions of general chit chat, knowing all the time that at some point I had to bring the conversation to the separation. I cannot remember what I ate. I can remember where I was sat as I could look out at the car park. If I could have just buried my head in the sand and walked away I would, but I'd lived through that once when I was in the cult of Maggot.

It came to "the time" and I did get the response I expected. My younger sister's personality is such that she is very pragmatic and down to earth. It was obvious that she did not approve of my decision, but she did her best to acknowledge it. Inside I was churning.

My dream would have been that she may not agree with me but would have made it clear that she would be there for me if I needed her. That didn't happen. As a sovereign being I am now much more aware that her opinion is her opinion, and she is entitled to it. It didn't stop it hurting at the time though.

I left that get-together still upset and in turmoil, knowing that my decision was not approved of. I now recognise the years of having my confidence worn down and being under subversive control meant that it wasn't surprising that it took such a lot of courage to go against what I knew my husband wanted. In many ways I'm gobsmacked that I actually had the courage to do it.

The whole situation was tied into financial difficulties and the business struggling, along with the relationship issues with my husband. I felt shame for having invested my money in my business and having gone into debt for it. I felt the shame of the business not being as successful as I would have liked. I felt hurt at my husband not believing in me and my abilities. I felt shame at not having the courage to have discussed it reasonably with my ex. I now recognise that reasonable was never a word that was going to come into play when discussing these issues with him.

And all the time I felt accountable and responsible to everyone else.

I don't think my family was aware of the importance I placed in their opinion of me. I knew that my hubby would present them with his version of events. I knew that version would be presented in such a way that he could not be at fault. I knew that he had been systematically discussing my twin sister's influence over me with her husband. I knew he frequently criticised people to me and then never said anything to their faces and often said the opposite. He had been gaslighting me whilst installing concerns with others about my decision-making abilities and how he thought I was going into a cult again. He even had a name in mind. The blame for our breakup was not his fault. He could not be to blame … ever.

As I was making my decisions for the breakup, I felt alone and isolated. I knew that to some members of my family I would appear to be making a crazy decision.

Given my private nature and my fear of appearing stupid for making decisions that others thought unwise, given that I had been in a cult and felt shame for having been in it, I chose not to share my internal struggles, my nagging worries, my upset at the way my husband ignored me and made subtle and not so subtle put downs.

I did not share with many of my family, or friends, the internal struggle I was going through. I was one of the world's best mask wearers. I could be a chameleon and appear to be who I am not, for the sake of getting along. I could avoid talking about things close to my heart if I thought the other person was likely to denigrate it. I was not about to expose my core beliefs for scrutiny when they had been so expertly ridiculed by my husband.

The wound has now healed but the scarring from the separation is still somewhat tender.

I hope that you will take away from this how your perceptions about yourself, have an impact on the way you create anxiety. Part of my lessons from this particular phase of my life is learning who I am as an individual. What are the boundaries I want to set? Which are my core values that cannot be violated? I realised how much I had grown through writing this book when I was able to talk openly with my family about writing about the anxieties of being in a cult. I'll know I've fully succeeded when I can talk about my husband without an element of anxiety about their response.

Thoughts and beliefs from my worry monster

Other people's opinions matter.

Any beliefs that led to me feeling shame.

Being successful is more important than anything.

I am not allowed to make mistakes.

Other people's opinions of my husband invalidate mine.

Truths with which to slay my worry monster

I cannot please everyone.

I cannot please all the people, all the time.

Not everyone needs to "get" me or my wacky ways.

No one is obliged to approve of me – only myself.

It's ok to be unsure while taking action.

It's okay to grieve for what might have been.

ACTIVITY 7

Releasing anxiety/worry using the Energy Alignment Method.

This is a simple technique that can be used in a multitude of ways.

For this example I am using it to show you how to release the negative emotions and align with the feelings you want to access.

I remember when I first found this technique and put it into practice on my sister Lynda. (If you hadn't guessed by now, she is my guinea pig for many of my new learnings.)

Lynda had come to the office, and we were preparing to go and do some work in a care home that was in difficulty. She had experienced a rough time in her last job and said, "you'll have to do some work on me first."

I was so excited as I was on the fourth day of a free five day programme and said "I've got just the thing for you."

It was the releasing and aligning section of the 5 step process of EAM

I am going to give you 2 of the steps of this to ensure that we get rid of your anxiety and worry.

I want you to think about a situation that you experience anxiety in. Where in your body can you feel the anxiety?

(where is it? What does it feel like? Does it have a shape and/or a colour?

I'll give an example.

E.g.

I feel anxiety like butterflies in my stomach. Its like a churning black gooey mess.

Having got to the bottom of what anxiety feels like for you, its then time to release the feelings and the emotion.

You do this by standing comfortably. Feet shoulder width apart. Knees soft and relaxed.

And you then state the following

"I am ready to release this feeling of anxiety that is like butterflies in my stomach that is a churning black gooey mess. I release it from my energy in all forms on all levels and at all points in time." (take a deep breath and let it go)

And now repeat this another twice.

I remember the feeling of utter surprise the first time I did it and the feeling just disappeared.

Having released the crap it is now time to align to how you would like to feel.

The alignment statement is similar to an affirmation in that it needs to be stated in the positive.

So how would you like to feel? Use words that are meaningful for you.

E.g.

I want to feel calm, confident, and energised. (Choose your own words)

It is now time to align to the feeling and emotional state you want to be in instead of anxiety /worry.

Once again take up the relaxed stance and this time I would like you to raise your hands in the air like the Y in YMCA dance (Yes, I know I'm showing my age). This leaves you open to receive the energy you are aligning to.

Now make the statement

I am ready to align to feeling calm, confident and energised (state the words in a positive tone of voice with meaning and connection to the feeling.) I accept this into my energy in all forms on all levels and at all points in time.

Repeat the statement twice more.

And as you complete the third statement – take a nice deep relaxed breath and allow your arms to slowly come down to your sides.

And that finishes the process.

Good luck and please feel free to let me know how you get on, on my Facebook page

Chapter 8

Snapshots of Anxiety In The Covid Pandemic

Friday March 20th 2020.

I am at my office and Lynda, Harriet and myself are packing up what we will need to be able to work from home, knowing that the lockdown comes into full effect on Monday.

It was one of the most surreal experiences of my life. I was going to be staying with my daughter to support her working from home and me doing the same whilst we both cared for my 2 grandchildren.

The majority of my clothes and belongings were in the spare bedroom at Lynda's house as this was where I was officially based, having left my husband just 1 month prior.

My daughter Sarah worked part-time and so I also worked part-time. She worked from home in the morning, and I did my time in the afternoon. I have little memory of the actual work I undertook with Lynda and Harriet, as much of the time the regular afternoon zoom call was one of emotional support and discussing our perceptions of what was going on. And I mean mega emotional support.

My worry monster was using all of my concerns about freedom of speech, freedom of opinion, the state taking excessive control, a pandemic that wasn't a real pandemic, me not feeling able to speak to those who were believing the narrative, all led to feelings of major anxiety. I was worrying about the future and the direction the world was taking.

I do not know how I would have kept my sanity without those calls. Let me explain.

Lynda and I are both nurses and had lived through the swine flu epidemic and the measures introduced at that time. It was apparent to us that the covid pandemic numbers were not reflecting the reality and were skewed to create fear and worry.

This next statement may sound harsh, but life does have a 100 percent mortality rate and we all have to die of something. I checked the data on the national statistics web page. The actual overall number of deaths for the year were no higher than previous years.

What was apparent was the trauma the lockdown created in the care homes. Relatives were no longer able to visit and residents with dementia experienced dramatic downturns in their conditions. It still brings up anger and fury in me that this was allowed to happen. I could not believe it was being allowed to happen. It totally created massive dissonance in me. How do you live knowing that you are going along with something so wrong but not having the power to change it? I was an agency nurse, simply choosing to help out because of the pandemic.

So back to the upsets I faced.

I saw residents who were left to die on their own (i.e. without their family) or with only 2 members of their family present, and then only in the imminent stages of death. Insanity ruled. I did what I could in the circumstances to support the staff on duty. The rebel in me came to the fore, from that point of dissonance, but then was suppressed because there was little I could do. This elevated my personal stress levels. Not only was I horrified at what was happening but there was sweet Fanny Adams I could do about it in the care home.

It was during this time working as an agency nurse that it was then decreed that we had to wear masks during the full shift. I was supplied with one mask to wear throughout the shift. I was a qualified nurse and nurse teacher. I was fully aware that any mask is only effective for 30 minutes max. The government hadn't got the lucrative contracts for PPE fully sorted at the time, so either way it was sh*t. If you believe in the masks, you could worry that they were in short supply. If you knew they were a waste of time, (as I did) you could worry that people were being taken in, and wearing something that added a barrier to communication with our vulnerable dementia patients, who were already additionally stressed by the sudden absence of their relatives.

The staff were amazing in the way they worked under the most difficult of circumstances. Their priority was caring for the residents.

There was one shift in particular, where the other nurse who was supposed to be on duty with me had not come in. I called Lynda, my twin, to come in and support me (we were both doing agency shifts at the same care home).

She came in and the hug that we exchanged was magical, having not seen each other for weeks. We kind of recognised that if we were getting close to residents, we were also willing to get close to each other, whatever the directives.

Throughout the period of the first lockdown, I struggled to cope with the stupidity of the rules being forced on the care homes. It broke my heart every time I saw a resident so ill and their family being unable to visit. It broke my heart when I saw a demented resident struggling because they couldn't understand why a family member was no longer there.

The stress on the workforce was phenomenal. I have nothing but utter respect for the care home staff, who continued to give their absolute best in such crazy circumstances. The pressure on us all was incredible.

Additional stress in the homes occurred as the GPs and other external professionals refused to visit, and were advising care and treatments over the phone, afraid of visiting. The irony of how many times previously that giving advice over the phone had been frowned upon by local authorities and CQC alike was not lost on me. I'll never forget a GP coming to take a PCR test for one of the residents we suspected had covid. They were practically dressed in a hazmat suit. The staff were there with their masks and plastic aprons. The contrast of this was mind blowing. We were struggling with PPE, our residents were being left vulnerable, and if it had been a truly dangerous virus, it was very obvious that the staff were being sacrificed to the disease.

At home I knew I had conflicting opinions to my daughter. Her father was at risk due to a physical illness and the worry monster created by the media bulletins every night, kept her and him in a state of fear and worry about what could happen. It's easy to say you consider the numbers don't reflect a pandemic, but if you or a close family member are in the high risk group it puts a whole new perspective on things. I respected her choice, but found it incredibly difficult as she did not want to hear my alternative considerations.

I knew of families whose whole relationships had gone to wrack and ruin because of differing beliefs over this, and I didn't want that to happen to me. I am very proud to say that with a willingness to accept each other's opinions, without constantly talking about them, my daughter and I navigated our way successfully through the pandemic and lockdown.

I could write a full book on this aspect of my worries and how they were fed during that period, but that is not the purpose of this book. Suffice to say, we survived and even at times thrived. We were blessed in having amazing neighbours, amazing weather and a fence that could be removed so we could party in our own gardens and still have a conversation with the neighbours.

The pandemic raised the anxieties of many people, whatever their belief systems. The whole country experienced a sense of impending doom and worry for the future. That worry has been exacerbated by the way the whole event was managed. There remain underlying anxieties for many people. The whole world has changed, and we are all in the process of adapting to the new world. How we navigate these changes has a major impact on our emotional well-being. We are not designed to be in a state of permanent anxiety and on alert, so we all benefit by learning how to switch off the fight or flight response and to get our hearts and mind back into coherence. The activity at the end of this chapter helps with that.

Thoughts and beliefs from my worry monster

I am powerless to manage this situation. I am powerless!!!

Everyone else is against me.

I don't fit in

My opinion is irrelevant

Truths with which to slay my worry monster

I may not be able to change the situation, but I can take control of my reaction.

Other people are autonomous beings with the right to hold whatever opinions they choose.

This is not a personal reflection on me.

I have the courage and strength to navigate any situation.

When in doubt, just give things time.

ACTIVITY 8

Connect to your heart

This technique is based on that taught by Greg Braden in line with The HeartMath Institute and I call it connect to your heart.

It allows you to be in control of your own reactions.

There is now scientific evidence that the heart has its own specialist nerve cells that are separate to the brain. These cells mean that the heart has "memories" which are separate to those of the brain. Whilst counselling helps sort out the brain's perceptions, it does not always reach the memories within the heart.

Releasing the emotions that are trapped there and letting them go can have profound effects on your well-being.

Connecting to your heart is a simple technique that optimises your immune response and removes anxiety.

It creates heart and brain harmony.

The technique has 3 steps.

- Shift your focus
- Shift your breathing
- Shift your feeling

Begin by connecting to your heart. Do this by placing your hand on your heart. This enables you to shift your focus and connect with your heart energy. It allows awareness to go to your heart.

The next step is to become aware of your breathing. Allow it to gently slow down. Let your exhale be longer than your inhale. This moves your biology into the parasympathetic nervous system. Continue your awareness within your heart.

The final step is to shift your feelings to ones of gratitude. Allow the feeling of gratitude to ripple out from your heart.

In this moment you are choosing to harmonise the neural network between your heart and your brain. You are optimising your biology and promoting your immune system and healing response.

When practised regularly it allows you to create a feeling of safety and create a high level of self-regulation in times of stress.

The effect of connecting to your heart has an effect on boosting your immune system that lasts up to 6 hours.

As always please feel free to let me know how you benefitted from this exercise and join us on my Facebook group.

Chapter 9

Flying In A Post Covid World

It's May of 2022 and Mirav has informed me that they are no longer required to wear masks in Italy to go into bars and restaurants. That's fantastic, I said, now would be an ideal time for me to come and visit you. You can check over my book details and I can have a lovely break in Italy.

I set about finding a flight to her local airport in Brindisi, to discover that my local airports do not do direct flights. That means I have to travel to Gatwick or Heathrow. I am still in my lack mentality and so set about finding the cheapest flight, and come up with an easy jet early morning flight. It is that early that I need to travel through the night. I have considered driving down, but the cost of parking the car is going to be higher than the cost of the flights, and even if I book a hotel the night before I will be up and out of bed at 4am.

For some strange reason without having my partner to talk my decisions through with, I find it a struggle to think clearly and sensibly. I am in a spin about what to do. I feel overwhelmed by the smallest decisions. Logic has gone out of the window, and panic and fluttery tummy came in.

I realise now that I am used to making decisions based on others' needs and the notion that I can choose for myself is so outside my personal norm that I am totally out of my comfort zone.

The key thing I realise is that little decisions, which if I had been making them for me and my hubby pre-covid I would have very easily made, all of a sudden, I am unsure of. I am second guessing myself and then third guessing and then fourth guessing. I have lost the skills and forgotten the tricks that go with planning a trip abroad. How can I have become so anxious about a simple flight booking? I have booked flights dozens of times. I have travelled abroad 3 times a year for over 10 years, yet here I am panicking over minor decisions.

To add to all this, before I can go, as a "non-vaxed" person – (wtf - when did that division come into being, oh how I long for the days pre-covid when we were all just people), I have to complete a lateral flow test. I check online for what needs doing. Finding somewhere they are performed is an issue. I have no idea or insight into how this is done. I am no longer an "expert" on this game called travelling.

The effect of leaving my husband, having a business which floundered during the lockdowns, and living through 2 years of reduced social contact, with restrictions on our movements and lifestyle, have all made their impact felt. I have lost confidence in making simple decisions. Actions that once would have been so easy all of a sudden feel overwhelming. The uncertainty comes with a sense of living in a world gone mad.

Throughout the pandemic I have been going against the accepted norms, (I didn't wear a mask, I had no intention of being vaccinated), and this created a conflict for me as I was aware that in all conversations I was outside the norm. This left me feeling uncertain about being able to express my truth without fear of contradiction.

I digress, so back to my flight to Italy.

I don't share with anyone how I feel about my plans. My worry monster keeps me in a state of low-grade anxiety. Am I making the right decision? Am I being stupid by going to stay with someone whom I had only met over the internet? Will I get on well enough to spend a week with them?

It is now just 2 days to my flight. I have finally decided to travel to the airport by train. I have not yet picked up my train tickets. My lateral flow test is organised. My sister is booked to take me to the train station on the Wednesday evening before I fly.

At 05.37 I hear my phone ping with a message. I have stayed at my daughter's house to be there for the morning to assist in getting the kids organised for school. I look to see who is messaging at that hour and nearly have heart failure when I read the text.

"Important information: we're really sorry that your easy jet flight 8373 on 26.05.22 has been cancelled. To see the options available to you, please go to Manage Bookings on our website or our easyJet App."

I am now in panic mode. I'm committed to getting the kids organised for school as Sarah is going into work early. I'm committed to picking up my grandson at 3pm as Sarah is working late. I am also committed to a morning sorting my expenses out for the accountant for last year's accounts. So I'm feeling like "Oh sh*t when will I have time to get a flight organised?" I have a quick peek at the flights available to discover that the only direct flights now available on the day I want to travel are from Heathrow.

I've no idea how I am going to get it all sorted. My daughter advises me to forget about it till I have taken the kids to school as there is nothing I can do about it until then. This is true but it's also easier said than done, especially if you have my worry monster on your shoulder creating all kinds of doubts and asking all sorts of questions. Will I be able to get another flight? Will I get my money back for the return journey as well as the cancelled flight? Will I have to forfeit my train tickets If I don't end up travelling? Do I cancel the trip altogether? Does my travel insurance cover any of this?

What a f**ing nightmare!

I manage to function without stressing at the kids as I take them to school. My sister and I meet up and complete the details needed for the accountant. I decide I am going to the local travel agent to let them search for the plane flight as I'm struggling to decide what to do.

I've let Mirav know that the flight is being changed. She has made all her arrangements for that specific flight so I'm now worrying because it's not only me its affecting but others as well. She is naturally perturbed as she too has made all her arrangements based on the time I was due to arrive in Italy. I feel responsible, even though it's the flight company that has cancelled and I have nothing to do with the decision.

I'm now sat in the travel agent thinking I can offload my stress. Wrong again!! They are tied in with certain airlines and cannot access the number of flights that I can on line. So back to my home and getting sorted.

It is at this point that I have a "f*ck it" moment

I realise that I am worrying unnecessarily about money, (that worry monster again) even though I have more than enough in the bank. Why do I not think of myself as worth the money? Why am I feeding myself doomsday scenarios about money?

As soon as I make this decision, everything comes into alignment. I decide I will cancel the return flight as I no longer trust the airline. I pay double the initial cost for my flight, but I am now travelling at a much more reasonable time with a reputable company. I find the info I need to be able to change my train tickets (the ticket sales man at my local railway station gives me the direct number to contact Train Line.) I phone and make the necessary changes.

The universe has been looking after me when I have a mixed up the date for my lateral flow test which means I am still within the 48 Hours required before my flight takes off.

The test is amazingly simple, is quickly completed and I have my results within half an hour.

I am ready, or so I thought, but my worry monster isn't going to go away that easily. I have packed my case and it is going in the hand luggage. It is only as I am on the train, on the way to Heathrow, that I click I have packed my toiletries as though they are going in the hold; so when I got to security I have the experience of throwing out what I think is all my excess. I am in that much of a fluster that I totally forget about the gifts I am taking into Italy and that these include creams and potions. I get to security and my bag is directed to the section to be inspected. I think I've just forgotten the deodorant but discover I am well over the amount required. Talk about feeling like an idiot. The security man is incredibly kind and tries to resolve it by finding which will be the cheapest to throw away, however I have the gifts for Mirav, along with my favourite perfume. He is understanding of my plight and I am offered the option of putting my case in the hold. I am so stressed I just accept the option.

He clears the way for me to go and check my luggage in and then arranges for another member of the security team to be available to help me to bypass the long queues. I have totally messed up and yet I have found a kind soul to be the one to get me sorted.

All this because I have tried to save money by not checking my luggage into the hold. I thought I was being smart by not having a larger case. It is at this point that I recognised the anxiety I had been feeling about travelling alone and not being familiar with the way travelling is done in the post-covid era. I haven't been willing to acknowledge it but the universe, in its beautiful and magnificent way, had ensured that my out of conscious awareness anxiety would manifest a few obstacles to raise my awareness.

Awareness raised! Thankfully having recognised that my worry monster had been at play – the rest of the trip is uneventful. The joy of meeting my friend at the airport is utterly phenomenal and a friendship that began on the internet is sealed in person.

In summary this experience serves to show how living with and acknowledging our worry monster is an ongoing process. As we face new challenges in life and living, he can still, at times, surreptitiously sneak in there. Not as strong, not as disabling, but still there. He lets me know where my unhelpful beliefs are present. He lets me recognise them at play. And then by living with increased awareness I'm able to disempower him and move on.

Thoughts and beliefs from my worry monster

Travelling is too difficult.

I am helpless and life's a struggle

I make decisions based on others' needs

Covid has knocked my confidence

Truths with which to slay my worry monster

I have the courage and resources to navigate any experience.

Growth takes place in the unknown outside my comfort zone.

I am a sovereign being and able to make my own decisions on my behalf.

ACTIVITY 9

Take physical action

Once anxiety has taken over and you just don't seem to be able to calm down whatever techniques you want to try, one of best solutions is to physically use up the adrenaline and the adrenal hormones by taking physical action.

Physical activity can work as both a prevention and as a cure.

When we become anxious the body responds as though there is a threat. It releases the adrenal hormones which are required for fight or flight. Your blood is directed to your muscles and away from your central organs. (Essentially, your body is not interested in digesting your food while you are under threat, nor rejuvenating and replenishing).

If these surplus hormones are not used up it leaves the body in a heightened state, especially if your worry monster is in its full power and repeating over and over in your head all the things that are likely to go wrong. This stops the body coming back to its natural state and being able to regenerate and rejuvenate, and over long periods of time can lead to physical ill health.

Actions to confound the worry monster

- Go for a brisk walk, jog, or run
- Go to the gym and beat the hell out of a punch bag
- Go to your bedroom and punch your pillows. Feel free to scream if you want to.
- Get your favourite music on and dance, dance, dance.
- Have sex
- Throw a paddy but without hitting anyone. Stand and stamp and scream.

Do feel free to warn your family what you are up to, or they may think you're losing the plot.

If you are having panic attacks – this is not anxiety and I recommend you seek professional advice and assistance.

Conclusion

Here we come to the end of this little book on anxiety and my worry monster.

The exercises are the most precious things in this book. I have used each and every one at different times on my journey.

The monster has not totally disappeared, but he has been tamed and brought much more under my control.

So many of us have been living lives with a great deal of low-grade anxiety which plays in the background like a backing track, out of our conscious awareness.

It's time for us all to free ourselves of our worry monsters.

It is time for us to conquer, tame, and take control of them.

It is time for us to use the "thinking method" that creates anxiety, and transform it into a tool for creating an amazing future. We can do this by trading the "worry images" for those of the optimist and the sense of knowing that all will be well. It may take a little determination, and commitment, but I promise it is well worth the effort.

I wish you joy and love and most of all an anxiety-free life.

And as my grandson Tyler would say – Peace at last.

Additions

Snapshot my Blog on anxiety during the pandemic

If you've got through this lockdown and plandemic without experiencing some stress and anxiety you are most likely a spiritual ninja with such a strong connection to the cosmos that you see it all for what it is. Or maybe you're more like me, you have had periods of abject terror at what's happening, and have to remind yourself that it isn't the world but how we perceive it that is the biggest influence on us.

I don't know which heading you come under, but if you're at the start of your ascension or simply a standard human being you will probably fit one of the following categories at some time during the last 5 months.

Anxious about

- "the" virus,
- the loss of your contact with your family,
- spending 24 hours a day with your family
- shielding for 14 weeks and then being able to go out again,
- people wearing masks,

- having to wear a mask,
- people not wearing a mask,
  the inconsistency of when to wear a mask
- a pub having different rules to a beauty salon.
- the loss of your sovereignty
- the notion of Agenda 21
- the government taking over our lives
- being furloughed
- not being furloughed
- working on the front line in shops, care homes, or hospitals (I won't add GP surgeries as they seem to have managed to keep contact to the absolute minimum)
- going back to work
- having no job to go back to
- disagreeing with friends and family about the authenticity of the virus,
- about the quality of the information available
- which research study should you trust
- whether a vaccine is the answer
- compulsory vaccination

and all this just by the present situation we are in. Now throw in the ascension of planet Earth and all who reside on her, and boy are we on a joy ride.

Add all the normal stuff we can get anxious about on top of this and there's no wonder that many of us are living in a state of anxiety.

We have now come to the phase of coming back out into the world. (That is if they don't decide we are in a second wave and it's time to lockdown a second time.) The uncertainty and lack of control impacts all of us in one way or another and adds to the stresses.

ME AND MY WORRY MONSTER or BLOG ON ANXIETY

If you wanted to design a system for buggering up people's immune systems, you could not have done it any better. If you wanted to create a ride to instil fear and worry for the future, you could not have done better.

Whatever the cause of anxiety, the way in which our body creates it is the same, and something can be done to help reduce it. (I can tell you I've been putting some practice in to change my thinking, my physiology, and my beliefs throughout this last 5 months. Whilst hanging on to the knowledge that we can rise above and through this.)

I remember my feeling when I was expecting us to be coming out of lockdown and once again it was extended. That's when it hit me. That's when I felt an utter sense of helplessness, frustration and sheer anger at it all. I then had the option of holding on to that anger, that frustration and bringing my immunity down or do something about it.

I did something about it.

Then next came my beliefs about what is the world game at the back of all this.

As a spiritual practitioner I am aware the world is going through a raising of its vibration. How can I best support the world through this process?

As sure as heck it isn't by getting anxious, overwhelmed and losing faith.

I have found it so easy to slip into the fear of loss of control over my life at times.

I refuse to allow my body to be put under the duress of constant fear hormones that reduce my immune capacity. As a human animal I am amongst a species that has the blessing of a mind that create images, and it is these images (usually in my unconscious) that impact how my body responds. If the image triggers fear, then my body will produce the adrenal and cortisol hormones to prepare me to fight or run. Now these hormones will nicely dissipate if I have a fight or if I hit a punch bag for 10 minutes, or run a mile. I don't tend to do any of these three, though, I have felt like hitting an MP or 2 at times through this.

I refuse to be bullied into believing the mainstream media. I intend to uphold the bargain I agreed before birthing onto this planet and assist this world in its ascension. I have the utter faith that the universe will send me the divine guidance and strength and courage that may well be needed. I've said to several friends "no one warned us how dense these energies would be" until I got here, I did not have any insight into what it is to be human. and how dense and uncomfortable it can be.

As we move through this ascension we may have a wee bit more of the roller coaster to ride, but hey, let's hang on like crazy and choose to enjoy the ride.

Acknowledgements

A huge thank you to the universe for guiding me to fulfil my dreams and write this book. An even bigger thank you to the universe for sending me Mirav Tarkka to nag, kick ass, and keep me on target to get it finished. Without her, I believe it would still be a wish not a reality. Thank you Mirav for all your patience, expertise and guidance in how to get a book from idea to printed article.

Thank you to my family who have supported me throughout this endeavour, especially my daughter Sarah and my sisters Lynda and Anne.

Thank you to Tyler, my grandson, for the quote - Peace at Last

Thank you for everyone who has been involved in my awakening journey, for all those who created the tools and methods that are included in this book.

Thank you to Harriet for the editing. I could not have trusted it to anyone better.

Thank you to you, the reader, who has bought and read the book. You are the reason it came into being.

And last but not least. Thankyou to me for having the courage and the perseverance to take the action and get sh*t done.

With love W

Printed in Great Britain
by Amazon